DIESELS on the REGIONS

LONDON MIDLAND REGION

Plate 1 (below):   Class 45/1 No. 45121 emerges from beneath the magnificent roof of St. Pancras Station, and heads the 16.12 express to Derby on 6th May 1978.

Gavin Morrison

Plate 2: The condition of Stalybridge Station in 1979 was a credit to the railway staff and to the owners of the privately-run buffet. Pictured on 23rd June 1979 is a two car Class 108 unit, which has just arrived from Stockport on the shuttle service.

Gavin Morrison

DIESELS on the REGIONS

LONDON MIDLAND REGION

Gavin Morrison

Oxford Publishing Company

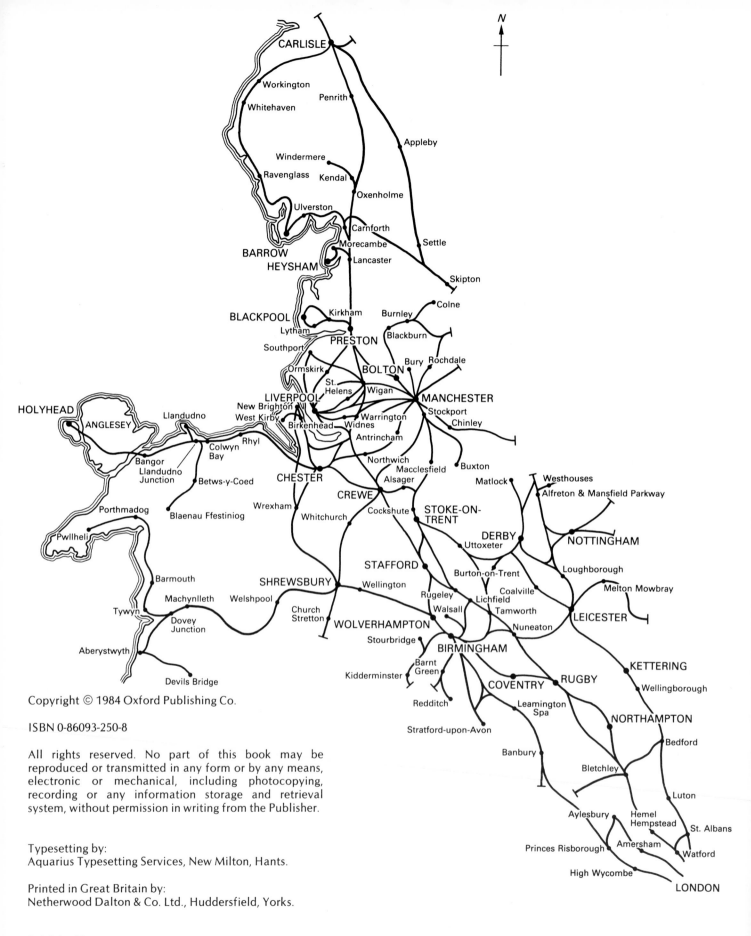

N

CARLISLE
Workington
Penrith
Whitehaven
Appleby
Windermere
Ravenglass
Kendal
Oxenholme
Ulverston
Carnforth
Settle
Morecambe
BARROW
HEYSHAM
Lancaster
Skipton
Colne
Kirkham
Burnley
BLACKPOOL
Blackburn
Lytham
PRESTON
Southport
Bury
Rochdale
Ormskirk
BOLTON
St.
Helens
Wigan
MANCHESTER
LIVERPOOL
Stockport
New Brighton
Warrington
Chinley
West Kirby
Widnes
Birkenhead
Antrincham
HOLYHEAD
ANGLESEY
Llandudno
Northwich
Buxton
Colwyn
Macclesfield
Westhouses
Bangor
Bay
Rhyl
Alsager
Matlock
Alfreton & Mansfield Parkway
Llandudno
Junction
Betws-y-Coed
CHESTER
Porthmadog
CREWE
STOKE-ON-
TRENT
Wrexham
Cockshute
Blaenau Ffestiniog
Whitchurch
DERBY
NOTTINGHAM
Pwllheli
Uttoxeter
Loughborough
Barmouth
STAFFORD
Burton-on-Trent
Melton Mowbray
Machynlleth
Welshpool
SHREWSBURY
Wellington
Tywyn
Coalville
Dovey
Church
Rugeley
Lichfield
LEICESTER
Junction
Stretton
Walsall
Tamworth
Aberystwyth
WOLVERHAMPTON
Nuneaton
Stourbridge
KETTERING
BIRMINGHAM
Devils Bridge
Barnt
RUGBY
Wellingborough
Kidderminster
Green
COVENTRY
Leamington
NORTHAMPTON
Redditch
Spa
Bedford
Stratford-upon-Avon
Banbury
Bletchley
Luton
Aylesbury
Hemel
Hempstead
St. Albans
Princes Risborough
Amersham
Watford
High Wycombe
LONDON

Copyright © 1984 Oxford Publishing Co.

ISBN 0-86093-250-8

Typesetting by:
Aquarius Typesetting Services, New Milton, Hants.

Printed in Great Britain by:
Netherwood Dalton & Co. Ltd., Huddersfield, Yorks.

Published by:
Oxford Publishing Co.
Link House
West Street
POOLE, Dorset

INTRODUCTION

To give a comprehensive photographic coverage of the London Midland Region in 96 pages is extremely difficult, as not only is the Region by far the largest, but also because main line diesel traction came to the Region at the start of nationalization, back in 1948, in the shape of the English Electric pioneers, Nos. 10000 and 10001.

My prime objective in compiling this book has been to give complete coverage of the Region, by making sure that such outposts as Aberystwyth, Whitehaven and Holyhead, etc. have been included, as well as the large and important centres on the Region.

After completing the selection of photographs, it was something of a surprise to find the wide variety of motive power which had been included, with many classes being featured which one does not normally associate with the Region. These include, for example, 'Westerns', 'Deltics', 'Warships' and Class 26 and 27 locomotives, in addition to the variety of diesel multiple units and railbuses, most of which have long since been withdrawn.

When assembling a diesel photographic album covering a specific area, it highlights the gaps in one's own collection, as well as making one realize all the superb locations which are now no longer available, due to electrification or, indeed, because of the rapid growth of trees and bushes.

Full integration of regional motive power is virtually now complete on the British Rail network, particularly as far as the London Midland Region is concerned, and one is now able to see virtually any class of main line diesel locomotive which still operates, working on this Region. Whilst this no doubt greatly assists the operating department, it is incredible to think that it took about sixteen years to achieve. I would like to take this opportunity to express my thanks to the photographers who have so willingly helped to fill the gaps in my own collection.

G. W. Morrison
March 1984

LONDON

Plate 3 (below): Class 40 No. D377 (later 40177) has just arrived at Euston with an 'up' express, amidst the advanced stages of the rebuilding of the station, in the summer of 1964.

M. Welch

Plate 4 (above): During its period on the West Coast Main Line, the prototype 'Deltic', resplendent in its pale blue and yellow livery, prepares to leave Euston with the 13.35 express for Perth in 1957.

M. Welch

Plate 5 (below): By 1964, the English Electric Co-Co locomotives, Nos. 10000 and 10001, were relegated to secondary duties and based at Willesden Depot. No. 10001 is seen waiting to leave Euston with an empty stock working to Willesden in the summer of 1964.

M. Welch

Plate 6 (above): 'Peak' No. D2 *Helvellyn*, later Class 44 No. 44002, is seen standing at Euston on 24th June 1964, after hauling a seven coach test train from Liverpool (Lime Street), a journey which it completed in 156½ minutes, averaging 74 m.p.h. The purpose of the test was to check track conditions and passenger comfort at electrification speeds prior to the completion of electrification.   *M. Welch*

Plate 7 (below): A familiar sight at Euston in the early 1960s was that of Class 40 locomotives, complete with headboards, at the buffer stops. The locomotives in this picture, taken on 5th July 1961, are believed to be No. D228 *Samaria* with 'The Merseyside Express' and No. D295 with 'The Emerald Isle Express'.   *M. Welch*

Plate 8 (above): Driver Pile of Camden, at the controls of English Electric Co-Co No. 10001, is ready to depart from Euston with the 13.25 service to Perth in 1957. No. 10001 was working in multiple with No. 10000. Note the LMS builder's plate. *M. Welch*

Plate 9 (above): Two Class 40 locomotives, with box headcodes, are pictured at the end of platforms 1 and 2 at Euston, after working 'up' expresses in 1962. *M. Welch*

Plate 10 (above): Type 1 No. D8000 (later Class 20 No. 20050) is ready to depart with empty stock for Willesden on 7th November 1960, whilst No. 10001 awaits the 'right away' with the 13.40 service to Bletchley. *M. Welch*

Plate 11 (above): On 16th September 1978, a Class 08 shunter, No. 08704, performs empty stock shunting duties under the wires outside Euston Station. *B. Morrison*

Plate 12 (left): Class 24 No. D5073 (later 24073) is ready to leave platform 8 at Euston with a 'down' parcels train in 1960. *M. Welch*

Plate 13 (right): A Derby Class 115 diesel multiple unit approaches the buffer stops at Marylebone, on 18th April 1983, with the 11.25 working from High Wycombe. The future of the station is believed to be uncertain, with the possibility of services being transferred to Paddington.

John Whiteley

Plate 14 (above): The bridge at the end of the platforms at Marylebone helps to frame this picture of a Class 115 diesel multiple unit leaving with the 12.10 service to Aylesbury, as well as keeping the photographer dry from the torrential rain of 18th April 1983. Note the very ornate platform lamps.

John Whiteley

Plate 15 (right): On 18th April 1983, the 12.10 train to Aylesbury is ready to leave Marylebone, and is made up of a Class 115 diesel multiple unit. Note the Advanced Passenger Train coach (APT) in the background.

John Whiteley

Plate 16 (above):   The first visit to St. Pancras of the Midland Pullman six car train, including two power cars, was for a press trip, prior to the introduction of the service on 4th July 1960. The Midland Pullman ran until 18th April 1966 when the first electric Pullman service started from Euston. The trains ran 'up' to St. Pancras from Manchester (Central) in the morning and returned in the evening, the stock being kept and maintained at Reddish Depot. This photograph of the Midland Pullman was taken in the spring of 1960.
M. Welch

Plate 17 (below):   On 6th May 1978, a Class 127 Derby suburban four car unit, with Rolls-Royce engines and hydraulic transmission, leaves St. Pancras with the 15.35 service to Bedford whilst, in the background next to the signal box, Class 45/1 No. 45121 awaits to depart with the 16.12 train to Derby.
Gavin Morrison

Plate 18 (above): The magnificent roof of St. Pancras Station dwarfs Class 45/1 No. 45102 as it leaves with the 17.16 service to Nottingham on 6th May 1978.

Gavin Morrison

Plate 19 (above right): No. D5387 was one of a batch of thirty six Class 27 locomotives which started their working life at Cricklewood. It is seen at St. Pancras after working in from Tilbury on 10th July 1962. In 1970, all the class was transferred to Scotland, with No. D5387 becoming No. 27104. This locomotive was again recently renumbered 27048.

M. Welch

Plate 20 (right): The 14.05 working to Sheffield, headed by Class 47/0 locomotive No. 47109, passes Cambridge Street Servicing Depot for St. Pancras on 23rd March 1975.

B. Morrison

Plate 21: The 'down' 'Robin Hood' express prepares to leave St. Pancras on 20th July 1962, headed by Class 46 locomotive No. D157, which subsequently became No. 46020.

M. Welch

Plate 22 (above): If ever there was a case for the preservation of a diesel locomotive, surely Nos. 10000 and 10001 were the favourite contenders. The two famous English Electric 1,600 b.h.p prototypes are seen surrounded by steam locomotives at Willesden Depot in 1960.

M. Welch

Plate 23 (right): An extremely interesting picture of Willesden Electric Depot, in May 1964, when it was being built, and which also shows the track layout at Willesden No. 2 box. Seen in the picture is a Class 24 with a 'down' local train, a Class 40 with a 'down' express and a pair of Class 20 locomotives with a parcels train from Kensington Olympia.

M. Welch

Plate 24 (left): Class 20 No. D8003 (later renumbered 20003) is seen, on 31st August 1957, at Devons Road Depot (Bow), when the locomotive was brand-new. The first Class 20 locomotives were allocated to this depot, which was the first to be dieselized on the London Midland Region.

B. Morrison

Plate 25 (right): A prototype three coach four-wheeled diesel rail-car, the leading driving brake being No. M79750, with a 125 b.h.p AEC bus type engine. The train was built by Associated Commercial Vehicles Ltd. and entered experimental service in 1953. After under-going regional trials it was put into regular service on the Watford to St. Albans, and Harrow to Belmont branches. It was replaced in 1958 by Park Royal bogie vehicles and, in 1960, was stored and eventually scrapped. This photograph shows the railcar at Bricket Wood in May 1954.

M. Welch

Plate 26 (below): A Class 105 Cravens twin car unit, fitted with AEC engines and built between 1956 and 1959, leaves Bedford (St. John's) with the 16.15 working to Bletchley on 9th May 1981.

B. Morrison

Plate 27 (above): A Park Royal four wheel single car railbus, No. M79971, enters Bedford (Midland) Station in 1959 with a local train from Hitchin. Built in 1954, these railbuses had 6 cylinder 150 b.h.p. AEC engines.

M. Welch

Plate 28 (above): A Class 122 Gloucester single car unit, No. 55009, built in 1958, stands at Watford and is ready to take up the 17.00 working to St. Albans Abbey on 30th June 1979.

B. Morrison

Plate 29 (above): On 16th June 1973, an empty stock working heads for London, past Elstree, with Class 25/1 No. 5187 (later 25037) and Class 25/2 No. 7522 (later 25172) in charge.

B. Morrison

Plate 30 (right): 'Peak' class locomotive No. D3 *Skiddaw* (later No. 44003) is seen near Elstow, south of Bedford, on 6th October 1959, working an 'up' morning Manchester (Central) to St. Pancras express. *M. Welch*

Plate 31 (below): On 21st May 1977, an Edinburgh to Margate special headed by Southern Region Class 33/0 No. 33049 leaves Brent Junction. The train had arrived from the North behind Class 47/0 No. 47202. In the background can be seen the flyover for the London North Circular road.

John Whiteley

Plate 32 (above): The 15.01 St. Pancras to Sheffield train approaches Kentish Town, on 21st May 1977, headed by Class 45/1 No. 45127. All the box head-codes fitted to Class 45/0 and 45/1 locomotives which remained in service at the beginning of 1983 have now been removed. *John Whiteley*

Plate 33 (above right): On 1st January 1979, the 10.05 Derby to St. Pancras train is seen approaching Harpenden Junction with Class 45/0 No. 45059 *Royal Engineer* in charge. The train consists of Mk. I steam-heated coaches, which no doubt accounts for the use of the Class 45/0 rather than the usual Class 45/1 loco-motive, prior to the introduction of HSTs in 1982/3. *John Vaughan*

Plate 34 (above): A pair of Class 28 Co-Bo locomotives, built in 1958 by Metropolitan-Vickers, and having Crossley 8 cylinder 1,200 b.h.p. engines, are seen passing Bedford with an 'up' morning Manchester (Central) to St. Pancras express in 1959. *M. Welch*

Plate 35 (left): A brand-new Class 127 Derby-built suburban four car unit is seen, on 11th August 1959, leaving Bedford for St. Pancras. These units, with 238 hp Rolls-Royce engines and hydraulic transmission, were introduced on this service in 1959 and have continued until the introduction of electric mul-tiple units. *M. Welch*

Plate 36 (above):   Running on the 'up' slow lines on 21st April 1982, a tanker train, headed by Class 47/0 No. 47290, approaches Oakley, three miles north of Bedford.

Gavin Morrison

Plate 37 (below):   An empty stock train proceeds northwards past Oakley on the 'down' slow line on 21st April 1982, headed by Class 45/1 No. 45105.

Gavin Morrison

Plate 38 (above): Approaching Aylesbury, on 15th February 1976, is a four car Class 115 diesel multiple unit, which was to form the 13.45 departure to Amersham.

B. Morrison

Plate 39 (right): Class 24 loco-motive No. D5016 (later 24016), plus an unidentified Class 20 are seen near Leighton Buzzard, on the West Coast Main Line, with an 'up' test train in the summer of 1959.

M. Welch

Plate 40 (left): No. 10201, built at Ashford in 1949, was the first of the Southern's main line diesel locomotives. In 1955, it was reallocated to the Midland Region and worked on the West Coast Main Line. It is seen in 1959 heading an 'up' fitted freight, near Cheddington.

M. Welch

BIRMINGHAM

Plate 41 (above): The empty stock forming the 13.15 service to Norwich, emerges into the sunshine at Birmingham (New Street) Station, on 25th August 1980, hauled by Class 31/1 No. 31305.
Gavin Morrison

Plates 42 & 43 (right & below): Two views of refurbished Class 50 No. 50038 *Formidable* when it visited the Birmingham area on 29th September 1982. Firstly we see it accelerating away from Birmingham (New Street), between Proof House Junction and Addesley Park, whilst hauling the 11.20 Liverpool to Paddington via Coventry and Leamington service. This was the return working of the 09.50 Paddington to Birmingham and Liverpool service, seen in the second view, slowing for Bordesley South Junction. Small Heath Station is just visible in the background.
John Whiteley

Plate 44 (above): On 29th September 1982 a Class 116 Derby-built diesel multiple unit, leaves Bordesley, with a Birmingham (Moor Street) to Shirley train.

John Whiteley

Plate 45 (right): Dominating the skyline, on 29th September 1982, are the cooling towers of Hams Hall Power-Station, as an unidentified HST unit, working the 06.46 Newcastle to Plymouth Inter-City express, approaches Water Orton.

John Whiteley

Plate 46 (below): The modern image of Birmingham International Station is clearly shown in this picture, taken on 28th May 1981, as Class 47/0 No. 47056 prepares to re-start the 14.23 Manchester (Piccadilly) to Portsmouth train.

Gavin Morrison

Plate 47 (above): Class 56 No. 56057 is seen passing Washwood Heath Sidings No. 1 signal box, on 29th September 1982, with a long train of empty merry-go-round wagons, which are returning from Didcot Power-Station to the Nottinghamshire Coalfield. *John Whiteley*

Plate 48 (below): A southbound coal train is seen at Saltley, on 2nd September 1982, headed by Class 31/1 No. 31132 and Class 25/1 No. 25051. The train is slowing down before stopping for banking assistance up to the Camp Hill line. *John Whiteley*

Plate 49 (right): A Class 31/1, No. 31251, joins the line from Birmingham (Moor Street) at Bordesley South Junction, from the Camp Hill freight line, on 29th September 1982, with a southbound train of empty coal wagons. The diesel multiple unit seen in the background is heading for Birmingham (New Street).
John Whiteley

Plate 50 (right centre): Class 56 No. 56009 heads a train of empty merry-go-round wagons, and is seen at Bordesley South Junction, returning north from Didcot, on the Western Region, on 29th September 1982.
John Whiteley

Plate 51 (below): Plenty of activity at Bescot Yard, on 29th September 1982, with Class 37 No. 37194 propelling a coal train into the south end of the yard as Class 47/0, No. 47076 *City of Truro* leaves with a Freightliner for Southampton.
John Whiteley

Plate 52 (left): A Park Royal two car diesel multiple unit, one of twenty built between 1958/9, each having two British United Traction (AEC) 6 cylinder 150 b.h.p. traction engines, passes LMS 'Jubilee' Class locomotive, No. 45631 *Tanganyika*, in the summer of 1960, as the unit enters Birmingham (New Street).
M. Welch

Plate 53 (below): An unidentified Class 47 locomotive stands in the sunshine at Birmingham (New Street), at the head of a bank holiday extra to the West Country on 25th August 1980.
Gavin Morrison

Plate 54 (right): The line between Coventry and Leamington has now been made single track. The 11.55 train from Paddington to Wolverhampton headed, on 11th April 1981, by Class 47/4 locomotive No. 47529, is seen passing the now closed station at Kenilworth.

John Vaughan

Plate 55 (below): A sight to delight the many 'Western' class enthusiasts. No. D1062 *Western Courier*, resplendent in maroon livery, is seen, on 3rd June 1963, leaving Leamington with an 'up' express for Paddington from Birkenhead. Happily, this locomotive is now preserved in this livery, and can be seen on the Severn Valley Railway.

John Whiteley

Plate 56 (above): The site of Aynho Station is the setting for this photograph, on 17th August 1982, of Class 56 No. 56050, heading for Didcot, with a train of loaded merry-go-round wagons from the East Midlands. The Birmingham to Paddington line can be seen in the background.

John Vaughan

Plate 57 (left): A recently refurbished Class 50 No. 50022 *Anson* is seen just south of Banbury, on 11th April 1981, with a diverted Birmingham (New Street) to Euston train. On this occasion, due to engineering work between Birmingham and Rugby, it is heading for Paddington.

Gavin Morrison

Plate 58: The 13.05 Manchester (Piccadilly) to Paddington (SuO) train makes an impressive departure from Banbury, on 13th September 1981, headed by one of the silver-roofed Class 47 locomotives, No. 47557.

John Whiteley

Plate 59: On 11th April 1981, one of the named Class 47/0 locomotives, No. 47077 *North Star*, heads south out of Banbury, and past a well-filled gasometer, with an 'up' Birmingham to Paddington express.

Gavin Morrison

Plate 60: Probably the only regular working for a Class 31 on a passenger train, on the Didcot to Birmingham main line at this time, was the 09.20 service from Reading to Manchester (Piccadilly), which is seen leaving Banbury, on 6th October 1979, headed by Class 31/1 No. 31294.

John Whiteley

Plate 61 (left): A regular working for Class 25s and, by 1983, one of the few passenger services scheduled for them was the 10.07 (SO) Aberystwyth to London (Euston) train. It is seen here, on 12th September 1981, restarting from Wellington, being headed by Nos. 25113 and 25139.

B. Morrison

Plate 62 (right): A Metropolitan-Cammell diesel multiple unit, pictured in original livery, enters Coventry with a working to Rugby during April 1962. These units were built between 1956 and 1959 and originally had 150hp ACE engines, which were later replaced by Leyland units.

M. Welch

Plate 63 (below): Class 25/2 locomotives, Nos. 25101 and 25286, wait for a clear road away from Nuneaton with a train of loaded hopper wagons.

B. Morrison

STOKE

Plate 64 (below):   The Class 25 locomotives had dominated the Cardiff to Crewe passenger services for many years until the Southern Region Eastleigh-based Class 33s took over in May 1981. Here, on 4th April 1979, No. 25063 is seen leaving Crewe with the 16.00 departure for Cardiff.

Gavin Morrison

Plate 65 (above): Class 25/2 No. 25157 emerges from under the impressive roof of Stoke-on-Trent Station, on 3rd July 1979, at the head of a local pick-up goods train. *Gavin Morrison*

Plate 66 (above): A mixture of diesel and electric power is seen on main line passenger duties at Stafford on 18th February 1979. Class 47/4 No. 47480 *Robin Hood* arrives with the 08.40 service from Liverpool (Lime Street) to Birmingham (New Street), and passes the 10.05 Birmingham (New Street) to Preston train, headed by a Class 86 electric locomotive. *B. Morrison*

Plate 67 (below): The 07.50 Cardiff to Crewe working rushes through Whitchurch (Shropshire), on 19th April 1980, headed by Class 25/1 No. 25063. Note the two white stick-on discs on the locomotive which denote an express passenger working. *John Whiteley*

FOCUS ON CREWE

Plate 68 (right): On 4th April 1979, a two car Class 101 Metropolitan-Cammell unit uses the through line at Crewe, whilst working as empty stock, before reversing back into one of the bay platforms at the north end of the station and working to Chester.

Gavin Morrison

Plate 69 (below): A Euston to Holyhead relief train is entrusted to Class 40 No. 40153, on 18th September 1982, much to the delight of the enthusiasts in the leading coach. Passenger workings from Crewe to Holyhead had been dominated by Class 47 engines for several years, whilst the Class 40 workings down the North Wales Coast, up to 1982, mainly originated from the Manchester Division and the Eastern Region.

John Whiteley

Plate 70 (above): Class 40 loco-motive No. D224, in original livery, and before being named *Lucania*, is seen arriving at Crewe whilst heading a heavy 'down' Euston to Manchester express in 1960.

M. Welch

Plate 71 (right): On 4th April 1979, a 'down' Freightliner train, headed by Class 47/4 No. 47451, hardly appears to be running at a profit as it approaches Basford Hall on the southern outskirts of Crewe just before entering the goods yard.

Gavin Morrison

Plate 72 (below): Motive power for the Crewe to Cardiff services is normally provided by Class 33/0 locomotives. On 18th September 1982, No. 33006, with the 16.02 departure for Cardiff, passes Class 86/2 electric No. 86230 *The Duke of Wellington* which is waiting to take over an 'up' express.

Gavin Morrison

Plate 73 (right): A fine study showing the original liveries for Class 40 and Class 47 locomotives. The picture was taken at the south end of Crewe and shows No. D341 (later 40141), and No. D1723 (later 47540) awaiting their next duties.

M. Welch

Plate 74 (left): A fascinating view of the north end of Crewe South Motive Power Depot, on 7th April 1961, photographed from the roof and showing, in the foreground, LMS shunter No. 12032, built at Derby in 1939, and English Electric prototype 1,600 b.h.p. No. 10001, which was built in 1947. A Hudswell Clarke shunter, No. D2509, fitted with a Gardner 204hp engine, is also present, together with many steam engines.

M. Welch

Plate 75 (right): 'Warship' class locomotives from the Western Region were a regular sight at Crewe during the 1960s, when they took over trains from the North to the West Country. Built by the North British Locomotive Company, No. D859 *Vanquisher*, waits to depart with the 12 noon Manchester to Plymouth train on 2nd August 1963.

M. Welch

Plate 76 (above): One of the Class 120 Swindon cross-country units which were built between 1957 and 1960, is seen leaving Shrewsbury with the 15.40 service to Swansea on 4th October 1980. Note the headlight, between the two front windows, which was fitted to these units in 1970 for operating on the Central Wales line.

Gavin Morrison

Plate 77 (above): A three car Class 120 Swindon cross-country set, working the 15.26 service from Chester to Wolverhampton, is framed in the window of the disused signal box at Coton Hill goods sidings, Shrewsbury, on 4th October 1980.

Gavin Morrison

Plate 78 (above): The Cambrian main line can be seen trailing off to the right, as Class 25/2 No. 25245, passes Sutton Bridge Junction, Shrewsbury, on 14th February 1981, with the 07.50 Cardiff to Crewe train.

Gavin Morrison

Plate 79 (above): Class 43 No. D854 *Tiger*, a North British-built 'Warship' locomotive, leaves Shrewsbury, on 23rd June 1962, with the 12.25 Manchester (London Road) to Plymouth Express. The picture is dominated by the magnificent signal box.

John Whiteley

Plate 80 (right): Headed by Class 25/2 No. 25131, the 15.04 Manchester to Bristol parcels train leaves Shrewsbury in the pouring rain, on 12th September 1981.

B. Morrison

Plate 81 (left): The animal life of Church Stretton appears to be unimpressed by the immaculate turnout, by Plymouth (Laira) Depot, of Class 50 locomotive No. 50008 *Thunderer*, on 22nd September 1979, as it heads the Crewe Works open day special, from the West Country.

Gavin Morrison

Plate 82 (left centre): On 22nd September 1979, the signalman at Dorrington has been swift in resetting the home signal, as Class 47/0 No. 47061 rushes by with a twelve coach summer (SO) 09.50 Paignton to Liverpool service.

John Whiteley

Plate 83 (below): Class 33/0 No. 33002 pounds up the bank from Shrewsbury to Church Stretton and passes Dorrington, at the head of the 12.25 from Crewe to Cardiff on 13th June 1981. Ballast wagons are seen parked ready for use on the Sunday.

Gavin Morrison

Plate 84 (left): Class 42 and 43 'Warship' diesel-hydraulic locomotives were the first main line diesels to oust steam haulage from the Shrewsbury to Cardiff and Bristol main line. In this photograph, taken on 23rd June 1962, Class 42 No. D813 *Diadem* uses its 2,000hp at the head of the 15.10 Liverpool to Cardiff express as it passes Bayston Hill, on the southern outskirts of Shrewsbury.

John Whiteley

Plate 85 (right): 'The Marches Venturer' steam special, from Hereford to Chester, had to be rescued by Class 25/2 locomotives, Nos 25195 and 25161, on 7th October 1978, when the famous ex-GWR steam locomotive *King George V* failed. The thirteen coach train is seen approaching the bypass on the eastern side of Wrexham.

John Whiteley

Plate 86 (left): Mold Junction was a very busy marshalling yard in the days of steam, but is now only a shadow of its former self. Class 47/4 No. 47454 rushes past, on 15th July 1978, with an 'up' Holyhead to Euston express. In the background can be seen a row of terraced houses, in which the enginemen and other railway employees, no doubt, used to live. The steam depot was situated just to the left of this photograph.

Gavin Morrison

Plate 87 (right): The destination blind on this Derby Class 108 unit indicates Birkenhead North as it leaves Wrexham (Central) on 18th September 1981 but, in fact, passengers for Birkenhead will change at Bidston on to the Merseyrail electric service for the final mile of the journey.

B. Morrison

Plate 88 (above):   A Derby-built Class 108 diesel multiple unit is about to pass under the LNWR-built Chester No. 6 signal box, with a working from Shrewsbury on 15th July 1983.

Gavin Morrison

Plate 89 (below):   A fine panoramic view of the triangle to the west of Chester is obtained from No. 6 signal box. On 15th July 1978 Class 47/0 No. 47262 rounds the curve with a Euston to North Wales train. The diesel multiple unit depot seen in the background, is on the site of the old Great Western steam shed.

Gavin Morrison

Plate 90 (above): Class 25/2 No. 25153 is seen alongside Class No. 24087 at Chester Diesel Depot on 30th January 1977.

Gavin Morrison

Plate 91 (right): The 10.00 Euston to Holyhead working emerges from the first tunnel to the west of Chester Station on 28th April 1979, headed by Class 47/4 No. 47436.

John Whiteley

Plate 92 (below): The 12.48 Holyhead to Euston service, headed by Class 47/4 No. 47454, curves around Chester No. 2 signal box to the east of the station on 28th April 1979.

John Whiteley

Plate 93 (left): Class 24/2 No. 5143 (later renumbered 24143) waits patiently at Aberystwyth, on 4th October 1973, at the head of the 18.30 mail train, before departing on its long journey through the night to York.

B. Morrison

Plate 94 (right): The dereliction of the Cambrian line is evident, as a two car Class 101 diesel multiple unit, with Wolverhampton High Level on the destination blind, leaves Borth Station, on 26th June 1982, with the 18.20 service from Aberystwyth to Shrewsbury. The passing loop and all sidings have now been removed.

John Vaughan

Plate 95 (left) Class 25/2 No. 25296 and Class 25/3 No. 25320 power away from Aberystwyth, past Llanbadarn, at the head of the 14.00 Aberystwyth to Shrewsbury train.

John Vaughan

Plate 96 (right): A special duty for Class 24 locomotive No. 24035, on 11th May 1975, as it passes very slowly over the toll bridge near Penrhyndeudraeth with LMS 'Princess Royal' No. 6203 *Princess Margaret Rose*, en route from Butlin's Holiday Camp, at Pwllheli, to the Midland Railway Trust centre at Butterley.

M. Welch

Plate 97 (below): An all-blue Class 103 Park Royal diesel multiple unit, together with a white with blue stripes Class 101 Metropolitan-Cammell unit, form the 17.10 Pwllheli to Shrewsbury service which is cautiously crossing the wooden piers of Barmouth Bridge at 10m.p.h. on 23rd June 1982.

John Vaughan

Plate 98 (left): A damp summer Saturday, 11th July 1981, and the mist obliterates the Welsh mountains as a Class 47/0 locomotive, No. 47066, reverses a train of Freightliner wagons into a siding at Llandudno Junction. Conway Castle and the towers of the railway bridge are just visible in the background.
Gavin Morrison

Plate 99 (left centre): The 09.23 Holyhead to Euston train leaves Llandudno Junction, on 11th July 1981, with Healey Mills-allocated Class 40 No. 40197 in charge. The layout of this junction was considerably altered in 1983. *Gavin Morrison*

Plate 100 (above): The 13.58 Bangor to Manchester (Victoria) train, with Class 40 No. 40135 providing the power, passes between the major road works as it approaches Colwyn Bay on 24th July 1982. This location was once a four track section, but the land is now being used for the North Wales Coast trunk road. *Gavin Morrison*

Plate 101 (left): A panoramic view of Colwyn Bay, on 24th July 1982, with the Little Orme in the background, is the setting for this picture of Class 47/4 No. 47447, which is heading the 16.08 (SO) Llandudno to Euston train past Old Colwyn. The track had to be slewed to accommodate the new road.
Gavin Morrison

Plate 102 (right): On 11th July 1981, Deganwy, the intermediate station on the Llandudno branch, is the setting for this picture of Class 40 No. 40025 *Lusitania*, heading round the extremely sharp curve en route to Llandudno. In the background can be seen the Conway Estuary and many small craft, and the Conway Suspension Bridge, sadly now partly hidden from view by the new road bridge.

Gavin Morrison

Plate 103 (left): The summer Saturday extras on the North Wales Coast line in 1981 only had one regular diagram for a Class 25; the 07.35 Nottingham to Llandudno service and the 13.26 return working. Class 25/2 No. 25126 was diagrammed for the working on 11th July, and is seen approaching Llandudno against the backdrop of the Conway Hills.

Gavin Morrison

Plate 104 (right): Llandudno Station is a sleepy backwater for most of the year, but it comes to life on summer Saturdays. Class 40 No. 40131 disturbs the track weeds, at the head of the 13.53 (SO) working to York on 24th July 1982.

Gavin Morrison

Plate 105 (above): One of the places where the London Midland Region obtains ballast is Penmaenmawr where Class 40 No. 40150 is seen in the quarry sidings, ready to depart with a loaded train for Helsby Junction on 4th May 1983.

Gavin Morrison

Plate 106 (above): There is little room for the railway and road along this section of the coast, as the hills come right down to the sea. The hill above Penmaenmawr, on which can be seen the different quarry levels, dwarfs Class 25/3 No. 25309 as it approaches Penmaenmawr Station with empty ballast wagons on 4th May 1983.

Gavin Morrison

Plate 107: Class 40 No. 40150 emerges into the sunshine out of the short tunnel at Penmaenbach Point, on 4th May 1983, half way between Penmaenmawr and Conway, with a train of ballast from the Penmaenmawr Quarries.

Gavin Morrison

Plate 108 (right): Bangor Station has not altered dramatically over the years. This picture, taken on 4th May 1983, shows a Metropolitan-Cammell Class 101 two car set, forming the 17.17 service from Bangor to Llandudno Junction, alongside ex-works Class 47/4 No. 47468, which has arrived a few minutes early with the 13.00 Euston to Holyhead train.

Gavin Morrison

Plate 109 (left): On 4th May 1983, an evening Freightliner train from Holyhead, headed by Class 47/4 No. 47501, takes the centre road through Bangor on its way to Crewe.

Gavin Morrison

Plate 110 (right): Sealink ferry *St. David* dominates this picture at Holyhead, on 20th September 1983, of Class 40 No. 40035 *Apapa* and Class 47/4 No. 47476. The Class 47 locomotive had failed near Llandudno Junction whilst working the 09.30 train from Crewe, and No. 40035 was attached in order to haul the train to Holyhead. The failed Class 47 locomotive is seen being propelled out of the platform to the depot.

F. J. Bullock

NOTTINGHAM

Plate 111: Plenty of activity at the west end of Nottingham Station, on 19th June 1983, as a Class 101 Metropolitan-Cammell unit runs alongside a double-headed heavy coal train, hauled by two Class 20 locomotives, Nos. 20181 and 20135, working nose to nose as is usual. Note the variation in the postion of the British Rail emblem on the Class 20 locomotives.

Gavin Morrison

Plate 112 (above): A Toton-based Class 56 locomotive, No. 56063, climbs Sharnbrook Bank, on the Midland main line, at the head of a lengthy rake of merry-go-round wagons which is returning to the Nottinghamshire Coalfields after delivering coal to a London power-station. The four track section is clearly seen in this photograph, taken at mile post 55, on 23rd April 1982, which is on the easier gradients of the climb before the last 3½ miles of a 1 in 119 incline to the summit. The lines in the background are not normally used by passenger traffic.

Gavin Morrison

Plate 113 (left): The driver of the 'Master Cutler', the 17.20 service from St. Pancras to Sheffield, has a good view of Sharnbrook Summit as the train storms up the last mile of the incline on 23rd April 1982, with Class 45/1 No. 45122 in charge.

Gavin Morrison

Plate 114 (below): The bridge just to the north of Wellingborough Station provides an excellent photographic vantage point in both directions and, looking south, we see ex-works Class 45/1 No. 45117 leaving the station with the 15.16 St. Pancras to Nottingham train, on 16th August 1980. The location is particularly attractive, with the signal boxes and semaphore signals.

Gavin Morrison

Plate 115 (right): Class 25/2 No. 25093 finds itself pressed into service with an 'up' summer Saturday extra, on 16th August 1980, and is pictured passing Finedon Road signal box at Wellingborough. The ten coach train will, no doubt, slow down on the three miles of 1 in 120 gradient to Sharnbrook Summit.

Gavin Morrison

Plate 116 (below): On 16th April 1982, the photographer was fortunate in capturing the unique Class 56 No. 56042, which can clearly be seen fitted with Class 58 experimental bogies, as it passes the old steam shed buildings at Wellingborough with an 'up' Tarmac Co. train.

John Whiteley

Plate 117 (right): In August 1962, the 'up' Midland Pullman is seen near Wellingborough with the fill-in daytime return working between Nottingham and St. Pancras. The units were built by Metropolitan-Cammell in 1959/60, utilizing one North British 1,000 b.h.p. engine in each power car and GEC traction motors.

M. Welch

FOCUS ON LEICESTER

Plate 118 (left): Bank holiday Monday, 29th May 1978, and the yard at Leicester Servicing Depot is rather full of motive power. From left to right these are Nos. 45145, 31325, 25159, 31294, 25123 and 45056.

Gavin Morrison

Plate 119 (left centre): A recently refurbished Class 116 diesel multiple unit leaves Leicester with the 13.38 departure for Birmingham (New Street) on 16th August 1980.

Gavin Morrison

Plate 120 (above): The 09.50 Norwich to Birmingham (New Street) working was an unusually heavy train on Saturday 16th August 1980 which, no doubt, accounts for the use of two Class 31/1 locomotives, Nos. 31313 and 31176. It is seen approaching Leicester past Leicester North signal box.

Gavin Morrison

Plate 121 (left): The centre platforms at Leicester are undergoing some rebuilding as Class 45/1 No. 45129, still running with its original front, leaves with the 10.12 St. Pancras express on 16th August 1980.

Gavin Morrison

FOCUS ON KETTERING

Plate 122 (above): Seen through the splendid roof pillars, on 16th August 1980, Class 45/1 No. 45103 prepares to stop at Kettering with the 13.12 St. Pancras to Nottingham train.
Gavin Morrison

Plate 123 (top right): Class 45/1 No. 45133 roars past Kettering Station signal box with the 14.01 St. Pancras to Sheffield service on 16th August 1980. *Gavin Morrison*

Plate 124 (right centre): The 13.00 Sheffield to St. Pancras working passes through Kettering, on 16th August 1980, headed by Class 45/1 No. 45112 *The Royal Army Ordnance Corps.* *Gavin Morrison*

Plate 125 (below): The old-world charm of the Midland station at Kettering is well-shown in this picture of Class 45/1 No. 45129 as it arrives with the 15.10 Nottingham to St. Pancras train on 16th August 1980.

Gavin Morrison

Plate 126 (left): Class 47/3 No. 47316 pauses at the east end of Nottingham Station, on 5th May 1979, probably for a crew change, before setting off for Immingham with empty tankers.

Gavin Morrison

Plate 127 (below): For twenty years, the 'Peaks' have dominated the Midland main line passenger workings until finally being replaced by HST units in 1983. On 9th May 1982, Class 45/1 No. 45133 passes through the very scenic cutting at Barrow upon Soar with the 13.33 service from Sheffield to St. Pancras.

Gavin Morrison

Plate 128 (right): One of the very few 'Peaks' still retaining the box headcodes in 1980 was Class 45/1 No. 45127. This locomotive is seen, on 25th August 1980, with the 09.30 working from Birmingham to Newcastle, passing through Burton upon Trent.

Gavin Morrison

Plate 129 (left): The summer Saturday extra workings from the Nottingham/Derby/Leicester area to the East Coast resort of Skegness have produced interesting double-headed motive power for many years. On 25th August 1980, the 08.50 Burton upon Trent to Skegness train is seen passing Findern with two Class 20 locomotives, Nos. 20197 and 20171, in charge.

Gavin Morrison

Plate 130 (right): A regular Class 25 diagram up to 1981 was the 7.30 working from Nottingham to Llandudno. On 5th August 1978, the 13.00 returning working, seen approaching Derby from the south before reversing for the last leg of the journey to Nottingham, is hauled by Class 25/2 No. 25215.

Gavin Morrison

DOUBLE-HEADERS IN THE NOTTINGHAM AREA

Plate 131 (left): The summer Saturdays 08.35 Derby to Yarmouth train passes through Long Eaton, on the misty morning of 16th August 1980, headed by Class 25/2 locomotives, No. 25127 and 25137.

Gavin Morrison

Plate 132 (left): Double-heading is a common sight around the Toton area, and mainly involves Classes 20, 25, 31 and 37. Class 37s Nos. 37094 and 37064 are approaching Toton Yard, on 14th April 1981, with a heavy load from the Nottinghamshire Coalfield, and are seen passing Stapleford & Sandiacre.

John Whiteley

Plate 133 (left): Working back to their home depot, on 14th April 1981, are two Class 20 locomotives, Nos. 20006 and 20087, seen on the 'up' slow line with an assortment of empty coal wagons. They are pictured north of Stapleford & Sandiacre.

John Whiteley

Plate 134 (right): On 5th August 1978, signs of summer Saturday motive power shortage are in evidence, as two Class 31/1 locomotives, Nos. 31117 and 31149, are pressed into service on a Newcastle to Cardiff express, pictured leaving Derby.

Gavin Morrison

Plate 135 (below): A brand-new Class 45 'Peak', No. D47 (later No. 45116) is seen passing the works at Derby, on 25th September 1961, on its way for testing before entering service.

M. Welch

Plate 136 (below): A 'down' express from St. Pancras arrives at Derby, on 5th August 1978, as Class 25/2 No. 25215 leaves on the last leg of its journey with the 13.00 (SO) Llandudno to Nottingham train. The locomotive would have run round its train in the station.

Gavin Morrison

Plate 137 (left): A line-up of Class 44 locomotives, including Nos. 44005 *Cross Fell*, 44002 *Helvellyn*, 44007 *Ingleborough* and 44004 *Great Gable*, are seen at Toton Depot, on Sunday 11th July 1976, and will be required for freight train duties in the following week. Apart from the first three years of their life, when they worked passenger trains on the Midland and West Coast Main Line, these locomotives spent the rest of their lives working from Toton on freight.

Gavin Morrison

TOTON DEPOT

Plate 138 (right): Toton Depot can always be relied upon to produce a good variety of motive power, and it was here that a particularly impressive line-up was on offer on 8th July 1976, when five different designs were on show. From left to right are Class 20 No. 20195, Class 47/3 No. 47332, Class 44 No. 44002 *Helvellyn*, Class 45/1 No. 45113 and Class 40 No. 40114.

Gavin Morrison

Plate 139 (left): For many years, a familiar sight at Toton Depot, on a Sunday, has been the long line of Class 20 locomotives. On 23rd April 1978, the following locomotives, Nos. 20041, 20113, 20157, 20171, 20174, 20167, 20006 and 20008 were seen with Nos. 20048 and 20188 at the end of the line but not visible.

Gavin Morrison

Plate 140 (right): The introduction of the HST units, with the start of the summer timetable in 1982 on the North-East to South-West route, dramatically reduced the number of Class 45 and 46 diagrams on these lines. On 25th September 1982, the 10.20 working from Penzance to Newcastle is seen approaching Ambergate Junction.

John Whiteley

Plate 141 (below): On 13th August 1983, a cross-country Class 120 Swindon-built diesel multiple unit is about to join the main line at Ambergate Station with the 18.00 service from Matlock to Derby. Ambergate was once a triangle, and the line to Matlock was formerly the Midland main line to Manchester.

Gavin Morrison

Plate 142 (above): The 13.53 St. Pancras to Sheffield train sparkles in the evening sun, on 2nd October 1980, as it passes Clay Cross with Class 45/1 No. 45135 *3rd Carabinier* in charge although, unfortunately, the nameplate has been removed.

Gavin Morrison

Plate 143 (below): Nearly at the regional boundary, and two Class 20 locomotives, Nos. 20199 and 20075, carry out their usual duties as they head north with a heavy coal train at Clay Cross on 2nd October 1980.

Gavin Morrison

MANCHESTER

Plate 144 (below): Probably the most photographed Class 40 of all was No. 40106, which never ran in the standard blue livery and was always much in demand on railtours. Set against the panoramic background of the City of Manchester, No. 40106 passes Ordsall Lane, Salford, on 2nd September 1982, on one of its regular duties with a North Wales coast train, the train in this photograph being the 10.45 Manchester (Victoria) to Bangor service.

Gavin Morrison

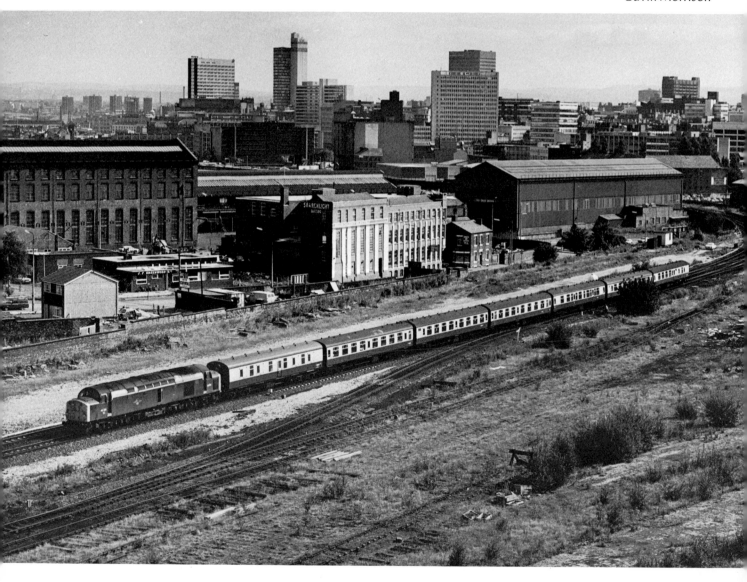

Plate 145 (left): The 15.15 Manchester (Piccadilly) to Harwich (Parkeston Quay) train, which was the return through working of the 07.17 departure from Harwich, has produced an interesting variety of motive power over the years in the form of Class 31, 37 and 40 locomotives. By 1980, Class 45/0s were the normal power and No. 45021 is seen ready to depart from Manchester (Piccadilly) on 20th August 1980. This service has now been integrated into the Nottingham to Glasgow workings and in 1981/2, Stratford's white-roofed Class 47 locomotives were regular performers.
Gavin Morrison

Plate 146 (below): On 2nd September 1982 Class 40 No. 40013 (formerly *Andania*) is seen inside Manchester (Piccadilly) at the head of the empty stock of the 'up' Manchester Pullman, which it has just brought in from Longsight Depot. This duty is normally an electric locomotive diagram.
M. Welch

Plate 147 (right): Two Class 101 Metropolitan-Cammell units form the 17.40 Manchester to Holyhead working, on 20th August 1980. It is seen passing through the disused station of Manchester (Exchange) on its 105 mile journey, scheduled to take 3 hours and 35 minutes. *Gavin Morrison*

Plate 148 (below): The splendid arched roof of Manchester (Exchange) Station has now been removed, and this has completely opened up the location photographically. In this view, taken on 11th February 1983, Class 40 No. 40001, with an Arpley to Healey Mills freight, has stopped for a crew change, whilst in the background, Class 47/4 locomotive No. 47444 *University of Nottingham* approaches Manchester (Victoria) with the 08.23 working from Glasgow Nottingham.

Gavin Morrison

Plate 149 (left): On 28th May 1980, the 09.30 Newcastle to Liverpool service was running so late that it was terminated at Manchester (Victoria) so that the stock and a Class 47/4 locomotive, No. 47426, could take up the return working. The locomotive and stock are seen passing through Manchester (Victoria) whilst carrying out the running round operation, with the train eventually reversing into the station.

Gavin Morrison

Plate 150 (below): The tracks in to the platforms at Manchester (Victoria), which are used by parcels and eastbound local services, do not appear to have had a visit from the weed-killing train for some time. On 20th August 1980, a Birmingham RC&W Class 104 unit is seen leaving, giving a spectacular exhaust display in the process.

Gavin Morrison

Plate 151 (right): Two Class 40 enthusiasts wait to ask the driver's permission to place an unofficial headboard on the green-liveried Class 40 No. 40106, before it departs with the 10.45 working from Manchester (Victoria) to Bangor on 4th September 1982. Their efforts were, in fact, successful.

Gavin Morrison

Plate 152 (below): During the last months of the 'Deltics' in 1981, they became regular performers on the York to Liverpool trains. As there was a 'Deltic' special virtually every weekend, the chosen locomotive was tested on the previous Thursday with the 08.50 York to Liverpool service returning with the 13.05. Three 'Deltic' locomotives, Nos. 55009, 55015 and 55022 were repainted for these specials, along with the National Railway Museum's locomotive, No. 55002 (painted green). No. 55022 *Royal Scots Grey* is seen passing Ordsall Lane, Salford, in the snow, on 17th December 1982, with a train that is hardly going to tax its two Napier 'Deltic' engines.

Gavin Morrison

Plate 153 (left): Class 55 'Deltic' locomotive No. 55022 (formerly D9000) *Royal Scots Grey* must have been giving problems with the 13.05 Liverpool to York working on 4th November 1981, as Class 45/0 No. 45005 was requisitioned at Manchester (Victoria) to assist. It is seen climbing Miles Platting Bank, with both locomotives actually working.

M. Welch

Plate 154 (above): The 09.00 summer (SO) Llandudno to York train was a regular Class 40 working for many years. Due to the reorganization of the North Wales coast trains, 1982 was to be the last year for this working. No. 40197 is seen emitting quite an exhaust as it crosses the viaduct at Droylsden, between Manchester and Ashton, on 11th September 1982.

Gavin Morrison

Plate 155 (left): On 11th September 1982, the 10.20 (SO) Manchester (Victoria) to Newcastle working is seen passing Ashton Moss North Junction headed by Class 40 No. 40056.

Gavin Morrison

Plate 156 (above): 'Deltic' No. 55002 *The King's Own Yorkshire Light Infantry* accelerates away from a permanent way slack as it approaches Mossley with the 08.50 York to Liverpool train on 29th October 1981.

M. Welch

Plate 157 (above left): A Class 123 Swindon Inter-City four car unit passes Midge Hill between Mossley and Greenfield, on 23rd August 1983, with the 15.57 Manchester (Victoria) to Hull working.

Gavin Morrison

Plate 158 (below left): Class 47/3 No. 47314 emerges from Scout Tunnel at Mossley, on 7th July 1979, with the then Saturdays only Bradford (Forster Square) to Manchester (Red Bank) empty vans train.

Gavin Morrison

Plate 159 (below): The ex-Saturdays only 09.00 Llandudno to York train is seen entering the cutting at Midge Hill, on 1st August 1981, with Class 40 No. 40182 in charge.

Gavin Morrison

Plate 160 (left): On 1st September 1981, Class 25/3 No. 25286 emerges from the cutting at Saddleworth, and passes the distant signal for Diggle as it makes steady progress to the summit at Standedge Tunnel with a 'down' freight.

John Whiteley

Plate 161 (below): Nothing now remains of the once busy yard at Diggle where, on 26th June 1982, the signalman keeps a watchful eye on the 15.00 Scarborough to Liverpool train, as it passes through headed by Class 45/0 No. 45069. The entrance to Standedge Tunnel is just visible behind the bridge in the background.

Gavin Morrison

Plate 162 (above): Due to engineering work on the Hope Valley line, on 25th February 1983, a Class 123 Inter-City unit is seen passing Guide Bridge with a Manchester to Sheffield working, and is being diverted via the now closed Woodhead route. *Gavin Morrison*

Plate 163 (right): On 10th June 1982, Class 40 No. 40001 joins the electrified main line at Heaton Norris Junction, Stockport, with a tanker train which has come from Guide Bridge, and is probably heading for Stanlow. *Gavin Morrison*

Plate 164 (below): Longsight has been the main diesel locomotive depot in the Manchester Division for many years. In this picture, taken on 25th February 1979, from left to right are seen Class 40 No. 40098, Class 25 locomotives Nos. 25131 and 25093, Class 47/3 No. 47352 plus a Derby lightweight refurbished Class 108 diesel multiple unit. *Gavin Morrison*

Plate 165 (left): A lucky picture, taken on 26th January 1982, of two Class 40 locomotives at Skelton Junction, near Altrincham. No. 40145 hurries along with a westbound freight working for Warrington, while No. 40094 waits in the loop before running round its cement train and heading east for Earles Cement Sidings, in the Hope Valley.

Gavin Morrison

Plate 167 (below): The merry-go-round workings from Healey Mills to Fiddlers Ferry Power-Station are now operated by Class 56 locomotives, and are currently routed over the Standedge line. On 27th April 1982, a very dirty, new-liveried No. 56092 is seen approaching Skelton Junction with a loaded train.

Gavin Morrison

Plate 166 (above): The I C I Tunstead to Northwich hopper trains were monopolized for many years by Class 25s. Classes 47, 45, 40, 37 and 20 are now regular performers. In this photograph, No. 25201 is seen near Skelton Junction heading for Northwich on 15th April 1982.

Gavin Morrison

Plate 168 (above):   The now-closed Kearsley Power-Station makes an impressive background to this picture of Class 47/4 No. 47413 passing the station with the 15.40 Nottingham to Glasgow express on 27th July 1982.

Gavin Morrison

Plate 169 (below):   On 28th September 1980, a shaft of sunlight catches the unique Class 40 No. 40069, the only member of the class having a cutaway body, as it approaches Bolton from the east with a very mixed freight.

Gavin Morrison

Plate 170 (above): The 'up' Sundays 10.42 Manchester to Euston working is seen climbing Moss Bank, near Macclesfield, on 16th August 1981, with Class 40 No. 40082 hauling Class 87 No. 87016 *Sir Francis Drake*, the power for the electric locomotive having been cut off due to engineering work.

M. Welch

Plate 171 (left): One of the short-lived Class 17 Bo-Bo Clayton diesels, No. 8598, is seen at Wilmslow in 1975 with the 'Wiggly Wire' test train. This train can have driverless control, and can operate from circuits laid down the track.

M. Welch

Plate 172 (below): When the Woodhead route closed on 18th July 1981, the remaining Class 76 electric locomotives were dumped at Guide Bridge and Reddish. All have now been sold for scrap, and the majority were dispatched during March and April 1983, mainly to scrap merchants in the Sheffield area. In this photograph, a batch of five Class 76 locomotives is being hauled by Class 37 No. 37130 past Bamford Station on the Hope Valley line, en route to Sheffield, on 29th March 1983.

Gavin Morrison

Plate 173 (right): An impressive line up of three Class 104 Birmingham RC&W units at Buxton, on 19th August 1979, all still fitted with two character headcode boxes. These units have been the backbone of the Manchester to Buxton services for many years.

Gavin Morrison

Plate 174 (right): A tanker train, headed by two unidentified Class 25 locomotives, is seen approaching Briggs Sidings, in 1977, on what is now the terminus of the former Buxton to Ashbourne line.

M. Welch

Plate 175 (below): On 3rd July 1979, the 18.15 Tunstead to Margam train climbs towards Peak Forest with Class 37 No. 37211 working very hard. A Class 25 locomotive pauses between shunting duties in the background.

Gavin Morrison

Plate 176 (left): Little now remains at Chinley to show what a busy place it used to be in steam days. With only two lines left in use, Class 25/2 No. 25101 passes the station, on 28th October 1982, whilst heading a Tunstead to Northwich I C I hopper train. *Gavin Morrison*

Plate 178 (right): An excellent location from which to observe workings on the ex-Midland Peak Forest main line, has always been the sweeping curve in the cutting at Buxworth. Probably the most impressive workings on this section are the daily 'Peakstone' hopper trains, which, in 1983, were occasionally double-headed by Class 40 locomotives. Two of the old 'Whistlers', Nos, 40104 and 40001, are performing the duty on 28th March 1983. *Gavin Morrison*

Plate 177 (below): Class 25/2 No. 25120 double-heads, with Class 25/1 No. 25060, on 28th October 1982, as they struggle up the 1 in 90 gradient at no more than 15 m.p.h. on the approach to Chinley Station, with a heavy oil train. *Gavin Morrison*

Plate 179 (left): The steam heating boiler is definitely operative on Class 47/0 locomotive No. 47051, on 22nd September 1979, as it climbs towards Chinley Junction with the Catering Car Centenary Express, whilst working from Manchester (Piccadilly) to Edinburgh.

M. Welch

Plate 180 (below): An extremely lucky picture in Buxworth Cutting, on 29th May 1980, as Class 40 No. 40145 descends the bank with an I C I hopper train, whilst Class 25/2 No. 25217 finds itself with the unusual work of piloting the National Railway Museum's Midland Single and Midland 4F, No. 4027, together with crane and coaches, back to the Midland Railway Centre at Butterley, after the 'Rocket 150' Celebrations at Rainhill.

Gavin Morrison

LIVERPOOL

Plate 181 (below):   The massive arched roof of Liverpool (Lime Street) dwarfs Class 47/4 No. 47406, which is pictured before it was named *Rail Riders*, as it waits for the signal to depart with the 14.05 service to Newcastle on 8th September 1979.

Gavin Morrison

Plate 182 (left): An immaculate ex-works Class 40 locomotive, No. 40135, stands under the wires at Liverpool (Lime Street), on 8th September 1979, at the head of the 15.05 train to York.

Gavin Morrison

Plate 183 (below): An enterprising move by British Rail (Eastern Region) was to organize two Trans-Pennine 'Deltic' workings on the last regular weekend of their operation on British Rail. This superb night shot shows No. 55009 *Alycidon*, suitably adorned for the occasion and sporting a 50A shed code, ready to leave Liverpool (Lime Street) in very wet conditions with the 19.10 departure for York on 27th December 1981. Happily, this locomotive is now preserved by the Deltic Preservation Group on the North Yorkshire Moors Railway.

John Whiteley

Plate 184 (right): Arriving at Edge Hill Station, on 11th September 1982, is a Class 108 two car unit. The station had been specially renovated for the 'Rocket 150' Celebrations to commemorate the opening of the Liverpool to Manchester line.

Gavin Morrison

Plate 185 (below): The Barrow to Liverpool trains are normally Class 47 hauled but, on 11th September 1982, veteran Class 40 No. 40013, formerly *Andania*, in its 23rd year of service, is seen leaving the spectacular sandstone cutting at Olive Mount, Liverpool, at the head of the 11.15 service from Barrow-in-Furness.

Gavin Morrison

Plate 186 (above): Only two sides of the triangle are now regularly used at Earlstown by passenger trains. Class 47/4 No. 47402, now named *Gateshead*, rushes past the ornate station buildings, on 23rd September 1981, with the 08.49 working from York to Liverpool.

Gavin Morrison

Plate 187 (below): Contrary to what it may seem, this photograph is not of a railtour, but is the normal 13.05 Liverpool (Lime Street) to York service train. Class 55 'Deltic' No. 55002 *The King's Own Yorkshire Light Infantry* is seen on 29th October 1981 approaching the bridge which was the centre of the 'Rocket 150' Celebrations at Rainhill.

Gavin Morrison

Plate 188 (above):   Class 40 No. 40143, with box head-code, leaves Springs Branch Yard with an 'up' mixed freight on 14th June 1982. The locomotive depot yard can be seen just under the bridge.

Gavin Morrison

Plate 189 (right):   A general view outside the old steam depot buildings at Springs Branch, on 18th August 1979, sees Class 25/1 locomotive No. 25047, Class 25/3 No. 25291 and Class 25/2 No. 25249, along with Class 40 locomotives Nos. 40076 and 40010.

Gavin Morrison

Plate 190 (below):   Cardiff-based Class 47/0 No. 47078 *Sir Daniel Gooch* races down the West Coast Main Line at Golbourne, on 14th June 1982, at the head of the 15.13 Manchester to Barrow train.

Gavin Morrison

Plate 192 (above): An interesting meeting at Ormskirk occurs when the diesel multiple units from Preston meet the electric multiple units from Liverpool (Central) on the same platform, with buffer stops in the middle. A through line is still in place, but is little used. Class 108 two car unit meets electric multiple unit, Class 507 No. 507024, before they both depart on 23rd May 1983.
Gavin Morrison

Plate 191 (above): Having delivered the loaded coal wagons and shunted the yard, on 12th May 1980, Class 25/2 No. 25119 leaves Southport Yard with empties returning to Wigan.
John Whiteley

Plate 193 (right): Taking a weekend rest at Birkenhead Depot, on 11th September 1982, are two Class 40 locomotives Nos. 40104 and 40061.

Gavin Morrison

Plate 194 (below): With Class 47/0 No. 47100 in charge, a short unfitted freight passes the ornate station buildings at Ellesmere Port on 11th September 1981.

B. Morrison

Plate 195 (below): A Class 03 shunter, No. 03170, is seen inside Birkenhead Depot, on 11th September 1982, as it is not required to work in the docks at the weekend.

Gavin Morrison

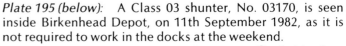

Plate 196 (above): Class 40 No. 40104 crosses the viaduct over the River Weaver at Frodsham, on 21st August 1982, as it heads an empty vans train for Manchester.

Gavin Morrison

Plate 197 (below): The petro-chemical complex at Stanlow can be seen in the distance in this view, taken on 21st August 1982, of Class 40 No. 40029 *Saxonia*, seen calling at Frodsham with the summer Saturdays only 13.58 service from Bangor to Manchester (Victoria).

Gavin Morrison

Plate 198 (left): A two car Class 108 unit, forming the 13.00 Manchester (Oxford Road) to Chester train, on 23rd February 1983, is seen crossing the River Weaver on the viaduct between Northwich and Greenbank. This is a steep gradient, and the I C I hopper trains from Tunstead are banked on this section. Note the signals controlling the locks on the river.

Gavin Morrison

Plate 199 (below): The 13.00 Manchester (Oxford Road) to Chester working is seen entering Northwich, on 22nd November 1982, with experimental Class 104 diesel multiple unit No. DM352. This former three car set has been made into a twin power car unit, but has one engine removed from each power car, giving considerable cost savings over the original formation. The unit is allocated to Longsight and the numbers are M50521 and M50446, although these units are to be numbered in a series from 78000. Class 40 No. 40061 can be seen leaving the depot to work a freight service to Warrington.

Gavin Morrison

Plate 200 (right): A heavily-loaded oil train heads down the West Coast Main Line to Winwick Junction, on 21st July 1981, with Class 40 locomotive No. 40030 (formerly *Scythia*) and Class 25/3 No. 25249 in charge.

Gavin Morrison

Plate 201 (below): On 10th July 1981, returning empty merry-go-round wagons from Fiddlers Ferry Power-Station pass under the West Coast Main Line at Warrington Bank Quay, with Class 47/0 No. 47198 ready to move forward to Arpley, before reversing into the goods yard and heading back north to Cumbria.

Gavin Morrison

Plate 202:   Framed by the roof of Hellifield 'up' platform, on 25th July 1979, Class 25/3 No. 25319 pauses briefly between shunting some empty ballast wagons, which it has just brought from the Carnforth area.

Gavin Morrison

Plate 203 (above left): On 22nd October 1981, a Cravens two car Class 105 unit leaves Blackburn on time, according to the station clock, with the 13.35 Preston to Colne service. Note the splendid Isle of Man Steam Packet Company's model boat in the showcase to the right of the front cab of diesel multiple unit.

Gavin Morrison

Plate 204 (above right): The telephoto lens picks out the 14.25 (SO) Blackpool to Leicester working, as it passes through Chorley Station, on 18th August 1979, headed by Class 47/0 No. 47040, the background being dominated by a very large gasometer.

Gavin Morrison

Plate 205 (left): The Preston to Colne service is entirely diesel multiple unit operated, as there are no run-round facilities at Colne. The 13.35 train from Preston is seen entering Burnley (Central) Station, on 4th September 1982, formed of a Class 108 unit.

Gavin Morrison

Plate 206 (right): Passengers awaiting the diesel multiple unit from Colne to Preston seem to be surprised to see Class 46 No. 46046 passing through Rose Grove Station, on 4th September 1982, at the head of a Newcastle to Bolton football excursion. The M65 motorway, seen under construction in the background, will pass through the site of the former steam depot.

Gavin Morrison

Plate 207 (left): In 1983, the only regular booked locomotive-hauled passenger train over the Copy Pit line, from Todmorden Hall Royd Junction to Gannow Junction, Burnley, was the summer (SO) 09.22 service from Sheffield to Blackpool and its returnworking. The line is also used by Blackpool Illuminations traffic and football specials, an example being Class 47/0 No. 47165, which is seen on North Wood Viaduct with a Leeds to Burnley 'Footex' on 9th April 1983.

John Whiteley

Plate 208 (below): On 30th June 1982, Class 37s Nos. 37221 and 37166, wind their way up the narrow valley past Portsmouth, towards the summit. The 6M32 Immingham to Preston Docks train of oil tanks needs to be double-headed up to Copy Pit Summit.

John Whiteley

Plate 209 (right): During the last five years, a great deal of engineering work has been carried out on the Trans-Pennine Standedge route on Sundays during the winter timetable, resulting in most of the Sunday traffic being diverted via the Calder Valley line. Class 47/0 No. 47088 *Samson* is pictured climbing towards Summit Tunnel, near Walsden, on 23rd September 1983, with the diverted 12.20 Newcastle to Liverpool express.

John Whiteley

Plate 210 (below): Cross Stone Church, situated above Todmorden, has a commanding view of the Calder Valley line in both directions. It stands out clearly on the skyline in this picture, taken on 24th May 1981, of an enthusiasts' special headed by two Class 25/1 locomotives, Nos. 25071 and 25064, heading east towards Hebden Bridge.

Gavin Morrison

Plate 211 (left): The Heysham to Haverton Hill I C I tank train is seen, on 12th December 1981, near Eldroth, on the Carnforth to Settle Junction line, in the winter snow, headed by Class 45/0 No. 45004 *Royal Irish Fusilier.*

John Whiteley

Plate 212 (below): Blackpool Tower rises above Blackpool (North) Station where Class 47/4 No. 47534 is ready to leave with an express for Manchester on 30th July 1979.

Gavin Morrison

Plate 213 (right): Two Class 31/1 locomotives are the regular motive power for the Tilcon trains from Swinden Quarry, on the Grassington branch. On 30th April 1979, Nos. 31226 and 31109 are seen ready to leave the quarry for Skipton, and, ultimately, Hull.

Gavin Morrison

Plate 214 (below): Only a month remained, when this picture was taken on 12th April 1982, for the Nottingham to Glasgow trains to run via the Settle to Carlisle route. The 10.20 service from Nottingham is pictured leaving Skipton, headed by Gateshead-allocated Class 46 No. 46004. Class 40 No. 40129, with box headcodes, awaits its next turn of duty in the bay.

Gavin Morrison

Plate 215 (above):   In 1982, the 15.37 train from Carlisle to Leeds usually consisted of four or five coaches, and was mainly hauled by a Class 31. Here No. 31126 coasts down the hill from Otterburn towards Bell Busk in the evening sunshine of 2nd September 1982.

Gavin Morrison

Plate 216 (above): The Class 47/3 No. 47318 will need to work very hard, on 5th September 1979, to haul this very long and heavy fertilizer train up the 15 miles of almost unbroken 1 in 100 gradient to Blea Moor Tunnel from Settle Junction.

Gavin Morrison

Plate 217 (below): On the beautiful evening of 26th August 1981, Penyghent stands out clearly as Class 47/4 No. 47578 climbs up the bank towards Horton-in-Ribblesdale with the 16.05 Nottingham to Carlisle working.

Gavin Morrison

Plate 220 (right): From above Moorcock Tunnel, there is a magnificent view across the Lunds towards Ais Gill. An unidentified Class 31 locomotive has just crossed Lunds Viaduct, on 10th August 1982, and heads south with the 15.37 Carlisle to Leeds train.

John Whiteley

Plate 221 (right centre): HSTs have travelled over the Settle to Carlisle route on several occasions, mainly during the East Coast Main Line diversions due to the collapse of Penmanshiel Tunnel. On 24th October 1981 an HST passes the sweeping curve at Armathwaite, after being used by British Rail for publicity photography.

Gavin Morrison

Plate 218 (above left)): The swan-song of the Settle to Carlisle line may well have been 2nd April 1983, as the West Coast Main Line was closed for engineering works at Tebay and all trains were diverted. Photographing trains passing on Ribblehead Viaduct has never been easy but, in 1983, it was truly remarkable. Class 47/4 No. 47518 heads the 07.45 Euston to Glasgow service and meets another Class 47/4 No. 47444 *University of Nottingham* with the 09.10 Glasgow to Euston train.

Gavin Morrison

Plate 219 (below left): A superb photograph of the ex-Mondays only Derby to Glasgow empty stock train, heading down Dentdale across the viaduct at Denthead on 26th October 1981. The unidentified Class 40 will have worked hard with the load of fifteen coaches on the climb from Settle Junction to Blea Moor.

John Whiteley

Plate 222 (right): On 3rd May 1982, Class 47/4, No. 47480, *Robin Hood*, is seen passing Birkett Common, which is situated between Kirkby Stephen and Ais Gill Summit, with the 11.50 Glasgow to Nottingham express. A fortnight later these services were withdrawn from the Settle to Carlisle line.

Gavin Morrison

Plate 223 (left): The little foot-bridge situated to the east of Grange-over-Sands has always been a popular spot from which to photograph the departure of 'up' trains. On 5th September 1980, the 11.00 service from Barrow to Euston is seen hauled by the regular motive power, a Class 47, on this occasion No. 47445.

John Whiteley

Plate 224 (below): An interesting comparison can be made between the present day scene at Lakeside & Haverthwaite Railway, and this picture, taken on 22nd August 1964. A Class 28 Co-Bo, No. D5708, is ready to depart with a train of non corridor stock.

Gavin Morrison

Plate 225 (below): A recently ex-works Class 47/4 locomotive, No. 47536, passes Plumpton Junction, on 2nd July 1982, with the 15.13 Manchester to Barrow train. The trackbed of the old line to Lakeside can be seen above the locomotive.

Gavin Morrison

Plate 226 (right): Two views on this page are taken from the same bridge, but looking in opposite directions. An 'up' merry-go-round train to Fiddlers Ferry Power-Station, headed by Class 47/3 No. 47316, passes the island platform at Ulverston on 2nd July 1982. The station seems to be under repair and, as it was early evening, it appears that the clock in the tower of the station buildings was not working.

Gavin Morrison

Plate 227 (below): A really splendid setting, under ideal photographic conditions, on 10th February 1983, with the tanks from Stanlow Oil Refinery, bound for Ulverston Oil Terminal, approaching their destination and being hauled by Class 25/2 No. 25229.

B. Morrison

Plate 228 (left): A merry-go-round train from a Cumbrian colliery, near Maryport, to Fiddlers Ferry Power-Station, near Warrington, passes along the single line section of the Cumbrian Coast line, near Netherton, on 11th February 1983, headed by Class 47/0 No. 47224.

B. Morrison

Plate 229 (below): Emerging from the tunnel at Whitehaven Station, on 2nd September 1980, is an unfitted freight hauled by Class 47/4 No. 47456. The station does not appear to have received a great deal of maintenance for many years.

Gavin Morrison

Plate 231 (above): Class 45s have never been frequent performers over Shap but the 'up' 'Waverley' Edinburgh to St. Pancras train was diverted off its regular path over the Settle to Carlisle route, via Shap, on 11th June 1962. No. D15, which became No. 45018 and is now withdrawn, is seen near Thrimby. Note the connecting door and box head-codes; a feature now removed from all members of this class.
John Whiteley

Plate 233 (below): Following serious problems with proto-type APTs, various alternatives are being considered. In August 1982, lateral force tests at various increased track cant deficiencies were being carried out over Shap. The curious test ensemble of two diesel HST units, Mark III coaches, and an APT electric power car in the centre are seen in Carnforth 'down' loop, on 11th August 1982, await-ing a clear road to Shap Summit. All power units were in action, involving the driver with two controllers for the two forms of power. 100m.p.h. was easily achieved up Shap and 131m.p.h. was reached near Tebay on the southbound journey.
M. Welch

Plate 232 (above): Prior to the electrification of the line, Class 40 No. D319 (renumbered 40119) rounds the sweeping curve at Low Gill with a long 'up' Edinburgh to Liverpool express on 18th August 1962.

Gavin Morrison

Plate 234 (below): The 'down' 'Royal Scot' storms through the cutting at Shap Summit, on 7th March 1970, headed by Class 50 No. D405 (later renumbered 50005 and named *Collingwood*). *Gavin Morrison*

Plate 235 (left): Carlisle, prior to electrification, was a photographer's paradise but with the overhead wires in situ, it now makes photography very difficult. A Class 108 refurbished diesel multiple unit arrives with the 15.55 service from Sellafield on 29th September 1982.

Gavin Morrison

Plate 236 (left): The collapse of Penmaenshiel Tunnel, on the East Coast Main Line, in 1979, caused widespread diversions. Some HST services were routed from Newcastle to Carlisle and Carstairs. On 15th August 1979, the mid-morning HST service from Aberdeen to King's Cross is seen arriving at Carlisle.

M. Welch

Plate 237 (below): A Class 26 locomotive, No. D5301, (now No. 26001) is seen on the night of 28th March 1966 at Carlisle Station, after arriving with a train from Edinburgh, which had travelled via the Waverley route.

John Whiteley